HOW TO MAKE CELERY JUICE FOR BEGINNERS

RECIPE FOR CELERY JUICE & THE TOP 10 BENEFITS OF CELERY

CARRIE MILLS

Table of Contents

CHAPTER ONE

JUICE OF CELERY

RECIPE FOR CELERY JUICE & THE TOP 10 BENEFITS OF CELERY

I made a startling discovery on our annual road trip to California. We couldn't find any organic celery in any of our local supermarkets! "What the heck is going on here?" What happened to all the celery? According to a friend, there is no celery because everyone is eating it. What? Why?

When I noticed that everyone was posting and sharing celery juice on social media, I knew the universe was conspiring against me. Podcasts devoted to health and well-being kept praising it. Seeing Celery Juice mentioned so frequently on social media convinced me to give it a go myself and see what all the fuss was about.

Currently in week three of drinking 16 ounces (2 cups) of organic celery juice first thing in the morning, I thought I'd let you in on my experience.

I'm not here to tell you what to eat or drink like I do with everything else on the blog. In the end, it's up to you to take care of yourself. Simply in case something piques your interest, I'd like to share some thoughts and possibilities with you.

Yes, to a large extent. Apigenin and luteolin, two powerful antioxidants found in celery, are the most important nutrients in the vegetable. Inflammatory diseases may benefit from apigenin and luteolin, which have been shown to reduce inflammation.

CELERY JUICE HAS THE FOLLOWING 10 BENEFITS:

A lot of evidence points to celery's healing properties, but as always, it's best to conduct your own research before making any conclusions. To see if you like it, just give it a go.

There are numerous cancer-fighting compounds in Celery Juice. Cancer cells can be killed by apigenin, a flavonoid in celery. Chemo-protective compounds found in celery's polyacetylenes have been shown to reduce the toxic effects of toxins while increasing immunity and slowing the growth of mutant cells.

restoring hydrochloric acid, which aids in faster digestion, celery juice helps heal and activate the gut. Celery juice aids in the production of stomach acid, which is essential for the digestion of protein-rich foods. For those who consume a lot of protein, this is a great supplement. In order to digest food, our bodies use up more energy if our stomach acid levels are low. This results in tiredness and a lack of energy. Preventing and healing ulcers and acid reflux by replenishing gastric mucus depleted by celery juice can be a significant benefit.

Celery Juice is a natural cholesterol-lowering agent. 3-n-Butylphthalide (BuPh) is a compound found in celery that has been shown to lower cholesterol levels, particularly LDL (bad cholesterol).

Natural anti-inflammatory properties of celery juice. Polyacetylene, a compound found in this product, eases the symptoms of gout, chronic joint pain, and rheumatoid arthritis. It is said to have calming and relaxing properties that extend beyond the physical body.

In addition, celery lowers blood pressure. Celery acts as a smooth muscle relaxant and improves the flow of calcium and potassium in cells, allowing blood vessels to expand and contract more easily, according to research findings.

The liver benefits from celery juice. Increased enzyme production in the liver is one of the ways celery juice works to improve liver health. Celery has been shown in studies to aid in the reduction of liver fat accumulation. Celery is rich in nutrients that protect the liver and actually aid in the production of enzymes that aid in the removal of toxins and fat from the body.

Increased circulation in the intestines aids digestion by promoting the movement of food through the digestive tract. As a mild laxative and diuretic, it can help with constipation, bloating, puffiness, and excessive water retention.

Sugar levels are lowered by drinking celery juice. Celery-derived compounds have been shown in studies to help lower blood glucose levels without increasing insulin levels.

The alkalizing properties of celery juice are well-known. Celeriac is one of the most alkaline-forming foods you can consume! An alkaline diet may help people live longer and stay healthier by reducing their risk of developing chronic diseases.

Celery juice is loaded with vitamins and minerals,

especially vitamin C. Folate, potassium, vitamin B6, vitamin K, and vitamin C are just a few of the nutrients abundant in celery. The skin's version of a cocktail. Celery contains luteolin, a compound that protects the skin from the inside and prevents UV damage. Celery's skin-healing properties have been hailed by some as a remedy for psoriasis and acne, as well as other skin conditions.

CHAPTER 2

IS CELERY AN EXTRAORDINARY VEGETABLE?

Yes, according to an article in Pub Med: "Celery has powerful antioxidant characteristics, to remove free radicals, because of compounds such as caffeic acid, p-coumaric acid, ferulic acid, apigenin, luteolin, tannin, saponin, and kaempferol." Different compounds and concentrations of celery have different healing effects, as is evident. Even the seeds of celery have a lot of nutritional value.

THE GUT IS HEALED BY CELERY JUICE?

CELERY JUICE: "One of the most potent and healing juices you'll ever consume. Every morning, on an empty stomach, sip about 16 ounces of fresh celery juice for a week to improve your health and digestion."

.

Organic celery should be used whenever possible. About 16

ounces is the approximate weight of a small bunch. He recommends making it every morning from scratch.

When making enough for two days' worth of consumption, I like to store any leftovers in the refrigerator and bring them to room temperature before drinking.

Is Celery Juice Safe to Drink?

For best results, take it first thing in the morning on an

empty stomach. Wait at least 20 to 30 minutes before consuming anything else, such as food or liquid.

SUGGESTED DRINK AMOUNT OF CELERY JUICE

Drink 16 ounces (about two cups, or a pint glass). If two cups are too much for you at first, try one cup and work your way up from there. Or, if it's unpleasant, it might not be what you need.

DO YOU HAVE TO USE ORGANIC CELERY?

• It's ideal, but it's not required. If you're using non-organic celery, be sure to thoroughly wash all of the stock to remove any pesticide residue. Celery is one of the most heavily sprayed vegetables on the market.

EATING CELERY INSTEAD OF JUICING IT: WHY NOT?

• It's possible. Even though celery is touted as a health savior, you'll need to eat the entire head (or bunch) in the morning to reap its full benefits.

When juiced, a whole head of celery (which contains 9-12 stalks) yields 16 ounces of juice.

INSTRUCTIONS FOR MAKING CELERY JUICE:

1.Organic celery should be cut in half and the stalks separated from the base.

2. Rinse them thoroughly in clean water to remove any traces of dirt or other contaminants.

3. Put the celery in your juicer and juice it up.

Drink right away.

Keep two bunches in a sealed mason jar for up to two days in the fridge.

BLENDER CELERY JUICE RECIPES:

1. To separate the celery stalks, use 1 bunch of organic celery and cut off the base.

2. Clean them with fresh water to get rid of any dirt or debris.

The celery stalks should be cut into 1-inch pieces and added to the blender with the remaining ingredients.

Add 1/4 cup of purified water to the blender and secure the lid with a rubber band. Blend until completely smooth.

Pour the blended celery through a clean nut milk bag that has been placed over the mouth of a pitcher or bowl. Squeeze the celery juice through the bag with your hands.

6. Drink right away, or make enough for two days (two bunches) and store in the fridge in a sealed mason jar for future use.

Is CELERY JUICE HEALTHY FOR ME?

Yes, to a large extent. Apigenin and luteolin, two powerful antioxidants found in celery, are the most important nutrients in the vegetable. Inflammatory diseases may benefit from apigenin and luteolin, which have been shown to reduce inflammation.

CHAPTER 3

CELERY JUICE HAS THE FOLLOWING 10 BENEFITS:

A lot of evidence points to celery's healing properties, but as always, it's best to conduct your own research before making any conclusions. To see if you like it, just give it a go.

There are numerous cancer-fighting compounds in Celery Juice. Cancer cells can be killed by apigenin, a flavonoid in celery. Chemo-protective compounds found in celery's polyacetylenes have been shown to reduce the toxic effects of toxins while increasing immunity and slowing the growth of mutant cells.

restoring hydrochloric acid, which aids in faster digestion, celery juice helps heal and activate the gut. Celery juice aids in the production of stomach acid, which is essential for the digestion of protein-rich foods. For those who consume a lot of protein, this is a great supplement. In order to digest food, our bodies use up more energy if our stomach acid levels are low. This results in tiredness and a lack of energy. Preventing and healing ulcers and acid reflux by replenishing gastric mucus depleted by celery juice can be a significant benefit.

Celery Juice is a natural cholesterol-lowering agent. 3-n-Butylphthalide (BuPh) is a compound found in celery that has been shown to lower cholesterol levels, particularly LDL (bad cholesterol).

Natural anti-inflammatory properties of celery juice. Polyacetylene, a compound found in this product, eases the symptoms of gout, chronic joint pain, and rheumatoid arthritis. It is said to have calming and relaxing properties that extend beyond the physical body.

In addition, celery lowers blood pressure. Celery acts as a smooth muscle relaxant and improves the flow of calcium and potassium in cells, allowing blood vessels to expand and contract more easily, according to research findings.

The liver benefits from celery juice. Increased enzyme production in the liver is one of the ways celery juice works to improve liver health. Celery has been shown in studies to aid in the reduction of liver fat accumulation. Celery is rich in nutrients that protect the liver and actually aid in the production of enzymes that aid in the removal of toxins and fat from the body.

Increased circulation in the intestines aids digestion by promoting the movement of food through the digestive tract. As a mild laxative and diuretic, it can help with constipation, bloating, puffiness, and excessive water retention.

Sugar levels are lowered by drinking celery juice. Celery-derived compounds have been shown in studies to help lower blood glucose levels without increasing insulin levels.

The alkalizing properties of celery juice are well-known. Celeriac is one of the most alkaline-forming foods you can consume! An alkaline diet may help people live longer and stay healthier by reducing their risk of developing chronic diseases.

Celery juice is loaded with vitamins and minerals, especially vitamin C. Folate, potassium, vitamin B6, vitamin K, and vitamin C are just a few of the nutrients abundant in celery. The skin's version of a cocktail. Celery contains luteolin, a compound that protects the skin from the inside and prevents UV damage. Celery's skin-healing properties have been hailed by some as a remedy for psoriasis and acne, as well as other skin conditions.

CELERY: Is This Superfood?

Because celery contains caffeic acid, p-coumaric acid, ferulic acid, apigenin and tannin, luteolin, tannin, and saponin as well as kaempferol as powerful antioxidants, it can help to remove free radicals. Different compounds and concentrations of celery have different healing effects, as is evident. Even the seeds of celery have a lot of nutritional value.

THE GUT IS HEALED BY CELERY JUICE?

CELERY JUICE: "One of the most potent and healing juices you'll ever consume. Every morning, on an empty stomach, sip about 16 ounces of fresh celery juice for a week to improve your health and digestion."

To get the most out of it, he recommends drinking it unadulterated.

Organic celery should be used whenever possible. About 16 ounces is the approximate weight of a small bunch. He recommends making it every morning from scratch.

When making enough for two days' worth of consumption, I like to store any leftovers in the refrigerator and bring them to room temperature before drinking.

Is Celery Juice Safe to Drink?

For best results, take it first thing in the morning on an

empty stomach. Wait at least 20 to 30 minutes before consuming anything else, such as food or liquid.

CHAPTER 4

SUGGESTED DRINK
AMOUNT OF CELERY JUICE

Drink 16 ounces (about two cups, or a pint glass). If two cups are too much for you at first, try one cup and work your way up from there. Or, if it's unpleasant, it might not be what you need.

DO YOU HAVE TO USE
ORGANIC CELERY?

• It's ideal, but it's not required. If you're using non-organic celery, be sure to thoroughly wash all of the stock to remove any pesticide residue. Celery is one of the most heavily sprayed vegetables on the market.

EATING CELERY INSTEAD OF JUICING IT: WHY NOT?

• It's possible. Even though celery is touted as a health savior, you'll need to eat the entire head (or bunch) in the morning to reap its full benefits. When juiced, a whole head of celery (which contains 9-12 stalks) yields 16 ounces of juice.

1.Organic celery should be cut in half and the stalks separated from the base.

2. Clean them with fresh water to get rid of any dirt or debris.

3. Put the celery in your juicer and juice it up.

Drink right away.

Keep two bunches in a sealed mason jar for up to two days in the fridge.

BLENDER CELERY JUICE RECIPES:

1.

1. To separate the celery stalks, use 1 bunch of organic celery and cut off the base.

2. Clean them with fresh water to get rid of any dirt or debris.

The celery stalks should be cut into 1-inch pieces and added to the blender with the remaining ingredients.

Add 1/4 cup of purified water to the blender and secure the lid with a rubber band. Blend until completely smooth.

Pour the blended celery through a clean nut milk bag that has been placed over the mouth of a pitcher or bowl. Squeeze the celery juice through the bag with your hands.

6. Drink right away, or make enough for two days (two bunches) and store in the fridge in a sealed mason jar for future use.

7.The impact of celery juice on my personal life:

This is not a call to embark on an extreme juice fast. I lean toward making small adjustments and observing how my body responds as a way to find a healthy equilibrium. As a whole, I believe the celery juice has been beneficial.

The speed and efficiency with which my stomach digests food has improved significantly after drinking celery juice in the morning for the past two weeks.

• My stomach feels flatter and I'm less bloated, and these effects last throughout the day.

• My skin is more hydrated and appears to be in better overall condition.

• I've noticed a decrease in my desire for salt and sugar.

• I feel nourished and healthy after drinking it - it has a calming effect on my body. I enjoy the way it makes me feel, so I'll keep drinking it. It's also delicious to me.

• I'm feeling more energized than usual.

The pain in my joints has decreased.

The best way to find out if it works is to just do it. It's up to you whether or not you like it. See if anything resonates with you in the following comments. Although many people have reported positive effects from drinking this, no two people are the same.

CELERY JUICE SHOULD BE DRANK BY WHOM?

For those who consume a lot of protein or suffer from low stomach acid, celery juice may be the answer. If you eat a lot of protein or fat, it may help to restore stomach acid, which is essential for digestion.

Finally, if Celery Juice is calling your name, don't hesitate! Let's see what happens. You may benefit from drinking it if it makes you feel better. If you experience any discomfort or have no effect, you may not like it!

You'll never know unless you give it a shot and put yourself through the ordeal. Is it right for you? If not, don't waste your time. You may not even be interested in it.

To be at our best, we know exactly what we need to do!

Listen!

THE END

www.ingramcontent.com/pod-product-compliance
Lightning Source LLC
Chambersburg PA
CBHW050620160726
48003CB00003B/1263